People Around Town

MEET THE PILOT

By Joyce Jeffries

Gareth Stevens
Publishing

Please visit our website, www.garethstevens.com. For a free color catalog of all our high-quality books, call toll free 1-800-542-2595 or fax 1-877-542-2596.

Library of Congress Cataloging-in-Publication Data

Jeffries, Joyce.
Meet the pilot / by Joyce Jeffries.
   p. cm. — (People around town)
Includes index.
ISBN 978-1-4339-9383-1 (pbk.)
ISBN 978-1-4339-9384-8 (6-pack)
ISBN 978-1-4339-9382-4 (library binding)
1. Air pilots—Juvenile literature. 2. Occupations—Juvenile literature. I. Jeffries, Joyce. II. Title.
TL547.J44 2013
629.13—dc23

First Edition

Published in 2014 by
Gareth Stevens Publishing
111 East 14th Street, Suite 349
New York, NY 10003

Copyright © 2014 Gareth Stevens Publishing

Editor: Ryan Nagelhout
Designer: Nicholas Domiano

Photo credits: Cover, p. 1 Monika Wisniewska/Shutterstock.com; p. 5 Andresr/Shutterstock.com; pp. 7, 15 iStockphoto/Thinkstock.com; p. 9 Stockbyte/Thinkstock.com; pp. 11, 21, 24 (airport) Comstock/Thinkstock.com; pp. 13, 19, 24 (airport) Top Photo Group/Thinkstock.com; p. 17 Digital Vision/Thinkstock.com; p. 23 Knumina Studios/Shutterstock.com; p. 24 (airplane) iStockphoto/Thinkstock.com.

Printed in the United States of America

CPSIA compliance information: Batch #CS13GS: For further information contact Gareth Stevens, New York, New York at 1-800-542-2595.

Contents

Pilots work in the sky!

They fly airplanes.

They first used
hot air balloons.

9

Some fly
big helicopters!

11

They land at airports.

13

They fly inside clouds!
Clouds are made
of water.

They stay in the nose of the plane. This is called the cockpit.

They take you
to many cities.

They move your
mail and boxes. This
is called shipping.

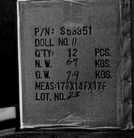

Many fly
in the air force.

23

Words to Know

airplane   airport   helicopter

Index